D1744405

Liturgy

for

Ordination:

The Series 3 Services

Introduction and Commentary

by

Michael Sansom

Tutor, Ridley Hall, Cambridge

GROVE BOOKS

BRAMCOTE   NOTTS.

CONTENTS

Copyright Michael Sansom 1978

THE DOCUMENTS

In the whole period of Alternative Services there have never been Series 1 or Series 2 Ordination Services.

Series 3 Ordination services were first published as a report from the Liturgical Commission (with the full title *Alternative Services Series 3 Ordination Services: A Report by the Liturgical Commission of the General Synod of the Church of England).* These were published by S.P.C.K. on 18 May 1977, with the coding 'GS 327', and the document is usually referred to here as 'The Report' or 'GS 327'. The Report was given 'General Consideration' in General Synod on 6 July 1977, and was then referred to a revision committee chaired by the Rev. Prof. D. R. Jones. This committee reported to Synod for the 'Revision Stage' in January 1978. The report of the committee is dubbed 'GS 327Y', and the revised text the committee proposed is dubbed 'GS 327A'. Neither of these documents is generally available. A few changes were made in Synod at the Revision Stage on 31 January 1978, and these, together with some minor consequential amendments subsequently made by the House of Bishops are recorded in 'GS 327B' (again not generally available). The services were then authorized in General Synod, at Final Approval Stage on 9 July 1978, for use from 1 September 1978 to 31 December 1979. During that period they will be 'adapted' for inclusion in the 1980 Alternative Service Book.

The services have not been published as glossy booklets like their predecessors in Series 3, and an application to include the text as an appendix to this Booklet has been refused (though the Ordination prayers themselves are included in Appendix 1). The full text is kept in duplicated form by the Secretary-General, General Synod, Church House, London S.W.1., and is made available by him to serious enquirers. Readers of this Booklet are therefore invited to write to him for a copy of the text.

The Ordination prayers are printed by permission of the S.P.C.K. on behalf of the Central Board of Finance of the Church of England.

THE COVER PICTURE . . .

. . . is by John P. Richardson. It does not commit author or publishers to a love of mitres . . .

First Impression August 1978

ISSN 0305 3067

ISBN 0 905422 38 4

INTRODUCTION

It should no longer be necessary to repeat the obvious remarks about liturgical revision, such as those about language and authenticity. According to Leslie Houlden, the commission responsible for the Series 3 Holy Communion rite were more concerned with liturgical than theological principles in their work.[1] To whatever extent we may be prepared to believe this assertion, it remains true that in the ordination services, cognizance has certainly had to be taken of theological factors, not least because of the relevance of the Ordinal to the Ten Propositions.[2] Here, above all, the task of revision has had to take place within a wider context than that of updating the services of the Church of England. As the introduction to the Report makes clear, the Liturgical Commission has taken into consideration the revised Ordinal of the Roman Catholic Church (1968) and the draft revision of the Episcopal Church of U.S.A. In addition to these, there is not only the Anglican-Methodist Ordinal of 1968, but also the debates on the nature of the ministry (reflected particularly in the ARCIC statement *Ministry and Ordination* and in the report *The Theology of Ordination*[3]) and on the diaconate (reflected in the ACCM reports *Deacons in the Church*[4] and *The Ministry of Deacons and Deaconesses*[5]). But the most important single influence of recent years has been the Ordinal of the Church of South India, which contains not only a form that has been a pace-setter but a preface stating clearly the understanding of the CSI of ordination and of the ministry.

[1] *Patterns of Faith* (SCM, London, 1977), p.2.
[2] See Appendix 2, p.28.
[3] Issued by the Faith and Order Advisory Group (GS 281).
[4] C.I.O., 1974.
[5] GS 344, 1977.

3

1. THE CONTEXT

(1) The Church of England and the Historic Practice of the Church

The notes appended to the services assert that 'the Church of England maintains the historic threefold ministry of bishops, priests and deacons' and refers further to Canons C1-4, relating to the ministry. It is embarrassing to find that the Canons perpetuate the unverifiable assertion of the Prayer Book Ordinal that 'from the Apostles' time there have been these Orders of Ministers in Christ's Church; Bishops, Priests and Deacons'—even if they do not contend that this is 'evident unto all men diligently reading Holy Scripture and ancient Authors'. The Canons are slightly more ambiguous, but at best it is clear that although three titles were current in the New Testament Church, two were used for the same office.[1] Even if there were three orders at an early date there is clearly no continuity of role between those offices in the practice of the early Church and in the practice of the Church of today. Nevertheless, the concept of a threefold ministry, inherited by the Church of England, has been maintained.

(2) The Debate on the Diaconate

The *status quo*, however, has been maintained because of the unresolved state of the debate about the shape of the ministry. Quite apart from the historical debate about the nature of the diaconate in the early Church, the modern diaconate has been the subject of intensive debate in recent years. Since 1878 the question of a permanent diaconate has been on the agenda of the Lambeth Conference, while the status of deaconesses has remained highly confused.

The 1958 Lambeth Conference issued a call to consider whether it would be wise to recover the diaconate as a distinctive order.[2] In complete contrast, an ACCM working party, reporting in 1974, advocated the discontinuance of the diaconate, proposing instead that each candidate for the priesthood should serve for a period of a year as a paid layman in the parish or sphere where he would begin his ordained ministry.[3] At the same time it urged the recognition of the status of deaconesses as lay ministers.

Further reflection and criticism, not least on the effects on ecumenical relationships, together with the resolutions of the Anglican Consultative Council led to the far less radical document *The Ministry of Deacons and Deaconesses* which concludes with three possible solutions, *viz.* (i) a *laissez-faire* approach, leaving the present situation as it stands, with the diaconate as a short, intermediate stage through which all candidates for the priesthood should pass; (ii) the abolition of the diaconate, which would clarify the status of deaconesses as members of the laity, ordinands serving

---

[1] cf. C. Jones, G. Wainwright, E Yarnold (eds), *The Study of Liturgy* (S P.C.K., London, 1978), p.293, n.l.

[2] *The Lambeth Conference 1958* (S.P.C.K., London, and Seabury Press, U.S.A.), pp.106f. The subsequent debate is conveniently summarized in *The Ministry of Deacons and Deaconesses* (GS 344).

[3] *Deacons in the Church*, p.34.

a year as paid laymen; (iii) an enlarging of the diaconate, so that a permanent diaconate would be created', for both men and women, but without recommendation concerning its stipendiary status, nor precluding the possibility of a deacon being later ordained priest.

That the report makes no recommendation is symptomatic of the general confusion. It is a confusion in the light of which the Liturgical Commission has been able to do no more than reflect the *status quo* of the Prayer Book, namely the threefold male order. Questions concerning the status of deaconesses and the ordination of women have had to be left on one side. In consequence there is no service for the office of deaconess, leaving the dioceses to continue to devise their own solutions to the problem.[2]

(3) The Ministry

Behind the debate about the diaconate, and indeed the debate about the offices which maybe exercised by women in the Church, lies a much larger debate concerning the ministry in which it is evident that much of the discussion revolves around the concept of *diakonia.* Powerful an influence as Hans Küng may have been on Vatican II, it was nonetheless a result of his dissatisfaction with the continued hierarchical orientation of Vatican II that he wrote *Why Priests ?*[3], which contains much of the thinking (including some direct quotation) behind his pronouncements on the Church in *On Being a Christian.*[4] While the ARCIC statement *Ministry and Ordination* is more concerned with the exercise of *episcope* in the Church and its relationship to the community (which it designates *koinonia*) the idea of the servant is the first to be cited in a brief review of the New Testament images of the minister.[5] Moreover, not only this document, but others, such as the Lutheran-Roman Catholic statement *Eucharist and Ministry,* the document from Les Dombes, *Towards a Reconciliation of Ministries,* and the agreed statement of the Faith and Order Commission of the W.C.C., *The Ordained Ministry in Ecumenical Perspective,* all conduct their discussion of the ordained ministry in the context of the ministry of the whole people of God.[6]

Thus it is clear that the current of opinion is flowing strongly against the idea of the ministry of the Church as concentrated in the hands of the professional ordained clergy. It is precisely in order to acknowledge the contribution of the laity to the mission of the Church that the revival of a permanent diaconate has been so widely canvassed, an office which would, presumably, cover a wide variety of forms of service.

[1] It was the repeated proposal of Vatican II that where it had fallen into disuse and where episcopal conferences deemed it opportune a permanent diaconate should be revived. *(The Documents of Vatican II* ed. Walter J. Abbott (Geoffrey Chapman, London, 1967), pp.55f., 380, 605).

[2] See footnote 4 p.21 below for one recent instance of a diocesan solution to this.

[3] Fontana, London, 1972.

[4] Collins, London, 1977.

[5] *op. cit.* para. 8.

[6] All four documents may be found in *Modern Ecumenical Documents on the Ministry* (S.P.C.K., London, 1975).

In addition to this trend towards acknowledgement of the ministry of the whole people of God, there has been a greater emphasis on the *diakonia* of the priesthood and the episcopate. One consequence of this has been an understandable, though not strictly logical, insistence that priests and bishops remain deacons even on ordination to the priesthood or the episcopate.

(4) The Ministry and the Ministries

The rediscovery of the ministry and mission of the whole Church has, however, sharpened the question of the nature of ordination itself. What sort of ministries make ordination appropriate, and what are the essential characteristics of the orders themselves? The Dogmatic Constitution on the Church *(Lumen Gentium)* continues to define the priesthood in terms of sacerdotal dignity, and to regard the episcopate as a high priesthood with special governing dignity. By contrast, the same document says of deacons that they are ordained 'not unto the priesthood, but unto the ministry of service[1]', defining their duties as those of administering baptism, acting as custodians and dispensers of the eucharist, assisting at and blessing marriages[2], bringing the viaticum to the dying, reading Scripture, presiding at worship and prayer, administering sacramentals, and officiating at funerals and burial services. In addition to this they are to be dedicated to duties of charity and of administration.[3] All of these features are reflected in the interim Ordination Rite of the Roman Catholic Church, with the interesting exception of the blessing of marriages.

The Series 3 services are in large agreement with the Roman Catholic order, viewing the deacon as an assistant to the priest and the priest as a colleague of the bishop, unhesitatingly ascribing responsibility for presidency at the eucharist to the priest. It could scarcely have run ahead of theological opinion and anticipated the outcome of the debate, but it is impossible not to draw attention to this feature in the face of the debate about lay presidency[4]. The clear point of divergence from the Roman Catholic order is the absence, both in the Anglican-Methodist Ordinal and in Series 3, of sacerdotal language. The relationship between priest and bishop, however, is less clearly defined than in the Roman rite.

(5) Ordination

What are the essential features of an ordination service? Cranmer, the probable architect of the English Ordinal, pruned away from the mediaeval rites of ordination those details which he regarded as peripheral to ordination. In this he was at one with the Continental reformers, replacing the complex ceremonies of the Pontificals with simple rites, consisting usually of the examination of the candidates and the imposition of hands accompanied by prayer. Paul Bradshaw argues a complicated case that Cranmer

---

1 *The Documents of Vatican II,* p.55.

2 One reason, traditionally, for excluding deacons from the solemnization of matrimony in the Church of England is that they should not be allowed to pronounce a blessing. (In fact, in law they *can* officiate and thus *must* pronounce the blessing).

3 *The Documents of Vatican II,* pp.55f.

4 cf. B. T. Lloyd (ed.) *Lay Presidency at the Eucharist?* (Grove Liturgical Study 9, 1977); A. E. Harvey, *Priest or President?* (S.P.C.K., London, 1975); H. Küng, *Why Priests?,* p.35; *On Being a Christian,* p.492.

may have drawn a distinction between the consecration and the appointing of a bishop, suggesting that by consecration he understood 'unction and similar ceremonies' and by appointing he meant 'ordination by prayer and imposition of hands.'[1]

This observation made, however, it is important to recognize that the concepts of ordination, imposition of hands and appointment are not quite as clear as at first sight they appear. In Cranmer's understanding appointment would seem to be constituted by ordination, whereas in *Apostolic Tradition* ordination and appointment are sharply distinguished, the former being reserved for bishops, priests and deacons, while the latter is reserved for those minor orders such as widows, readers, virgins and subdeacons. When we consider the Greek vocabulary associated with ordination, we find that *cheirotonia* is a general term used to signify appointing and so may mean no more than stretching out the hand in voting, but it may, by extension come to include the formal consequence of election, namely the laying on of hands. But although it is, apparently, never used in connection with any other ecclesiastical rite than ordination, it never means simply 'laying on of hands'; that action is signified by *cheirothesia* or *epithesis cheiron.*

It would appear that from an early date it was assumed that appointment to the major orders (=ordination) must normally be symbolized and effected by the laying on of hands. It is of course true that the imposition of hands may signify other things, but in this context its meaning is ordination.[2] That is not, however, to say that ordination is to be reduced to mere imposition of hands, since tradition has specified two other elements as essential, namely election and prayer.[3] Thus Hippolytus says

> 'Let him be ordained bishop who has been chosen by all the people, and when he has been named and accepted by all, let the people assemble together with the presbytery and those bishops who are present on the Lord's day. When all give consent, they shall lay hands on him, and the presbytery shall stand by and be still. And all shall keep silence, praying in their hearts for the descent of the Spirit . . .'[4]

In the Gallican order, the candidate for ordination is presented to the people, with the response *dignus est.* The Gallican practice was later adopted into Roman usage. Doubtless the actual election gradually became more formalized, but in the English Ordinals of 1550, 1552, and 1662 it exists only in the form of a requirement by the presiding bishop that any impediment to ordination should be alleged. Congregational approval is

[1] P. F. Bradshaw, *The Anglican Ordinal* (Alcuin/S.P.C.K., 1971), pp.15f.
[2] But see p.11 below.
[3] cf. Preface to C.S.I. Ordinal and introduction to GS 327, p.5.
[4] *Apostolic Tradition,* 2. (All references to *Ap. Trad.* will cite the paragraph numbering of Cuming's edition (Grove Liturgical Study 8, 1976)). See also Bradshaw's treatment of this passage in his essay 'ordination 'in G. J. Cuming (ed.) *Essays on Hippolytus* (Grove Liturgical Study 15, 1978).

signified by silence. In contrast to this, the rites of Series 3, following the lead of CSI, the Anglican-Methodist Ordinal and the Roman Pontifical, restore the verbal response of the congregation.

It has long been the custom of the Roman Catholic Church that the imposition of hands takes place in silence, the ordination prayer following, while the bishop stretches out his hands towards the candidates. Paul Bradshaw regards this practice as purely pragmatic, probably occasioned by the impracticality of repeating the ordination prayer for each candidate when there were numerous candidates. Presumably, he adds, the practice in the case of the bishop was a question of uniformity rather than of necessity. Again, according to Bradshaw, it was the mediaeval period that saw the birth of the formula *'Accipe Spiritum Sanctum . . .'* ('Receive the Holy Ghost . . .') in order to enrich the silent imposition of hands.[1] Thus in the English Ordinals, the imposition of hands is accompanied not by prayer, but by the formula 'Take thou authority to execute the office of a deacon . . .' in the case of a deacon, and 'Receive the Holy Ghost, for the office and work of a Priest . . .' in the case of a priest, while that for a bishop simply substitutes the word 'bishop' for 'priest'.

In practice the effect is twofold. First, ordination appears to consist of the laying on of hands accompanied by exhortation instead of prayer; and secondly the unfortunate impression is given that the deacon requires no gift of the Holy Spirit for his office, beyond the conviction that he is called to it. All he requires is authority, without further defnition of the nature of that authority. The service for deacons is all the more unsatisfactory because the relationship between prayer and ordination is even less clear than in those for priests and bishops.

It is scarcely surprising, therefore, that dissatisfaction with 1662 and the failure of the Anglican-Methodist unity scheme have tempted some dioceses to try their hand at improving the Ordinal, even if most of the changes have been on a very modest scale. In the light of this and of its relevance to the Ten Propositions, the Series 3 services are long overdue.

---

[1] *op. cit.* p.4. Until, and even after the researches of the French Roman Catholic Jean Morin, published in 1655, the formula was widely regarded as the essential form of ordination (*Ibid.* pp.83f., *passim*).

2. PRINCIPAL CHARACTERISTICS

(1) A Standardization of Practice

In common with the Marriage and Funeral Services of Series 3, the Ordination services have been shaped to the pattern of the Series 3 Holy Communion rite. The Ministry of the Word follows a brief introductory section consisting of a greeting and collect and includes an Old Testament reading as well as Epistle and Gospel. The sermon follows the lections instead constituting a somewhat abrupt opening to the service, as it does in 1662 (which, of course, assumed that the service would follow Morning Prayer). The ordination service itself is taken up after the (optional) recital of the Nicene Creed.[1] In addition a proper thanksgiving, post-communion sentence and collect and blessing have been provided.

(2) A Uniformity of Practice

Perhaps the most obvious influence of liturgical revision to date is to be seen in the paragraph numbering, which gears coincidentally into Series 3 Holy Communion (note the rubric of para. 21 *'The Bishop resumes the Communion Service at the Peace',* which is, as the footnote points out, para. 21 of the Series 3 rite). This numbering of paragraphs reinforces the uniformity of practice found in the Series 3 Ordination services, but cannot itself be held to account for it. It will be readily seen that the CSI Ordinal, the Roman Catholic rite and the Anglican-Methodist Ordinal establish a uniformity of practice concerning the position within the service of the ordination of the candidates. No longer, in Series 3, are deacons ordained before the Gospel, while priests and bishops are ordained after it. This uniformity of practice in turn leads to a uniformity in the placing of the presentation, the declaration and the prayers. Nor is it simply a uniformity of pattern: the content of the service is, as far as possible, identical.

It has been a long standing practice that the newly ordained should symbolize the office to which they have been ordained by performing one of the duties of that office. So, in response to the bishop's words 'Take thou authority to read the Gospel . . .' one of the deacons reads the Gospel lection and, although the 1662 service does not explicitly envisage the participation of the newly ordained priest, it is in some dioceses customary for him to assist with the administration (and even 'concelebrate').

While it may be desirable that the newly ordained should participate in some way, there is no reason that the reading of the Gospel should be seen as a peculiarly diaconal responsibility that requires his ordination before reading the Gospel. If there were some reason, it might be more proper that he should be handed a book of the Gospels, as in the Roman Catholic rite[2], instead of a New Testament. Even if it is regarded as the deacons' specific responsibility, it remains true that relatively few congregations have a deacon at all, let alone a steady stream of deacons. Indeed, so many churches have only one ordained member of staff, that the reading of the Gospel is either yet another task fulfilled by him, or else it is delegated to a lay member of the congregation.

[1] The Creed follows the ordination of priest in 1662, but precedes the ordination of bishops. It is specifically excluded from the Roman Catholic rite, but included in the Anglican-Methodist Ordinal.

[2] But not in order that he should read the Gospel, since the liturgy of the Word up to and including the Gospel precedes the laying on of hands.

It may still be appropriate for the Gospel to be read by one of the candidates, but it could be read equally by a candidate for the priesthood (who would, unless a permanent diaconate were established and the present arrangement abandoned, be a deacon anyway) or a candidate for the diaconate. Candidates for the priesthood can without great difficulty be involved in the administration of communion; indeed, there is no reason why deacons should not be similarly involved, as they are in the Roman Catholic rite.[1] The question of concelebration, however, may be another matter altogether. It is a practice that is not particularly edifying, to say the least, and the general 'atmosphere' of Series 3 Holy Communion (I avoid the term 'theology' in deference to Leslie Houlden) would appear to render the concept otiose. If we have learned nothing else from the rite, we should at least have learned to accept back into our vocabulary Justin Martyr's term 'president'. It is more than a mere question of terminology, since the switch from 'celebrant' to 'president' underlines the priest's function as one of the whole celebrating congregation. Strictly speaking, it is the whole congregation that concelebrates; the priest is a member of the congregation performing a presidential function.[2]

Together with the uniformity of practice in the position in the service of the ordination, we should note the uniformity of practice in the declaration, where Series 3 follows the lead of the CSI Ordinal in incorporating the homily as the opening section of the Declaration in the service for priests. It then parallels the opening section of the Declaration in the services for deacons and bishops. In each case, then, the Declaration begins with a consideration of the tasks of the office to which the candidates are to be ordained.

(3) The Essence of Ordination

It is clear from the Series 3 services that those aspects which seemed to the early Church to be essential to ordination, namely election and the imposition of hands accompanied by prayer, are at the heart of the matter. We shall examine later the form of the election; suffice it now to observe that it is a practice which has been re-established in Anglican thinking by the CSI rite and the Anglican-Methodist Ordinal and there is no doubt that it is a feature which commends itself strongly over against the clericalized Prayer Book service.[3] As much to be commended is the congregation's acceptance of their obligation to support those who are to be ordained in their ministry.

[1] All this suggests that it is in fact difficult for the newly ordained actually to exercise their distinctive ministry within the ordination service. After all, what is a new bishop to do?

[2] It is only within a more sacerdotalist framework that this view may not make sense.

[3] We must note that E. C. Ratcliff concludes from a study of the versions of *Ap. Trad.* that election is not necessarily *by* the people. The Ethiopic, Sahidic and Arabic versions all read 'from the people'. Ratcliff suggests that the ceremony in which the Gospel book, held open over the bishop's head, recorded in *Apostolic Constitutions* and *Epitome,* is intended to indicate the passage of Scripture held to have indicated the Lord's choice. He sees here a continuation of the procedure of election by lot (Acts 1.23-26) which preserves the divine initiative, but adds 'No doubt it is the right and function of the *laos* to "put up" . . . any whom they believe to be morally and spiritually "vescovabili".' (*Liturgical Studies,* ed. A. H. Couratin and D. H. Tripp (S.P.C.K., London, 1976), p.159). Cf. Bradshaw's essay 'Ordination' in *Essays on Hippolytus.*

When we turn to the laying on of hands we find that in contrast to the Roman Catholic rite, it is accompanied by the words, said over each candidate 'Send down the Holy Spirit upon your servant *N* for the office and work of a deacon (priest/bishop) in your Church' leaving aside both the Roman Catholic rite's silence and the old imperative formula. In this way it becomes clearer that ordination is the work of God, not a matter of a legal formula administered by a bishop or under his control. Moreover the prayer is identical for each order, an innovation which has the merit of recognizing the propriety of seeking the Holy Spirit's empowerment of the deacon for his office as much as of the priest and the bishop for theirs. Curiously, however, the Prayer Book custom of singing *Veni Creator* at the ordination of a priest or bishop but not at the ordination of a deacon is retained. There seems no good reason for this omission, either liturgical or theological, even though it is ancient. Its inclusion would add to the conviction that the office of a deacon *does* require the equipping of the Holy Spirit which the prayer at the laying of hands implies.

(4) Doctrine

It was the request of the Bishop of Peterborough to the revision committee that the services should contain no change in, nor diminishing of, doctrine implicit or explicit in the 1662 Ordinal and also that they should be acceptable to the Roman Catholic, Orthodox and Old Catholic communions. The committee expressed the view that they were satisfied that the services met such requirements, adding that they had been shown to experts representative both of the Free and the Roman Catholic Churches.[1]

As has already been remarked, the Commission had little option but to preserve the existing situation in respect of the threefold ministry. Nevertheless it is noteworthy that Acts 6.2-7, the 1662 alternative epistle for the ordination of deacons, has been dropped. It clearly has nothing to do with the ordination of deacons as we know them, and its retention would have been totally inappropriate.[2] But the change is symptomatic of an attempt, to be seen in other services also, to move away from the proof-text use of Scripture, seeking justification for the orders directly from the New Testament. Thus 1 Tim. 3.8-13 (1662 and CSI deacons' rite), 1 Tim. 3.1-6 (1662 bishops' rite) and Acts 20.17-35 (1662 and CSI bishops' rite) also disappear. Curiously, however, Mal. 2.5-7 has been added by the revision committee as an alternative Old Testament lesson for the ordination of priests. In view of the general attempt to select readings which express the calling of God and the Church's offering of itself in the mission and ministry of the gospel, it would seem to be a somewhat injudicious choice. Indeed, the only lections which would appear to have chosen been with the order in mind, are the Gospel for the ordination of priests (John 20.19-23)[3] and

[1] GS 327Y, §7.

[2] Indeed, the passage does not even include the word 'deacon', though the cognate verb is there, which presumably gave rise to the tradition.

[3] It will be remembered that Jn. 20.19-23 conserves the wording 'whose sins you forgive, they are forgiven' etc. In the Anglican-Methodist ordinal it was included not only in the Gospel, but also at the giving of the Bible 'be mindful of the words of the Lord Jesus to the apostles which you heard . . .'. But *were* the words to the apostles especially? At any rate, the Gospel alone retains the words now.

the Old Testament lesson for the ordination of a bishop (Num. 27.15-20, 22)[1]. In general, however, it may be seen that the services move towards a view of the ordained ministry within the context of the ministry of the whole Church.

That being said, and recognising that the concept of *diakonia* informs all three services, it must be added that the Psalm portions might have been better chosen. The passage for the ordination of deacons[2] is a prayer for understanding, guidance and obedience, for the ordination of priests[3] an assertion of the desire to praise God and tell of his marvellous works, while that for the ordination of a bishop[4] opens with an assertion of the petitioner's obedience. Read together they give a somewhat triumphalist effect, beginning, as it were, with diaconal abasement and ending with episcopal glory. It seems a pity that Psalms were not chosen to express more clearly the praise or prayer of the whole Church.[5]

A further indication of the shift in emphasis from the ordained ministry as such to the ordained ministry within the context of the whole Church is the congregational involvement in the election and in the congregation's pledging of itself to support those who are to be ordained. A further indication still may be the dropping of the original proposal for an opening sentence quoting Luke 10.2: 'labourers' are not to be thought of as restricted to the members of the ordained ministry.

Considerable debate has revolved around the use of the terms 'priest' and 'presbyter', the revision committee of Synod amending the title of the service for the ordination of priests to 'The Ordination of Priests or Presbyters'.[6] has long been recognized, even by Roman Catholics, that the term *presbyteros* is not to be translated into Latin as *sacerdos* and that the English 'priest' derives from *presbyteros.* The commentary prefacing the Anglican-Methodist Ordinal observes, however, that the term 'presbyter' is to be preferred, adding

> 'It is in fact confusing for theological discussion if the title "priest" is appropriated to the second Order of the historic Ministry, for in one main tradition of Christendom, ministerial priesthood is something common to presbyter and bishop.'[7]

However, despite the assertion of the commentary that some of the Anglican critics of the Ordinal were wrong in asserting that 'presbyter' is not a word of English or American usage, the revision committee nevertheless felt that the term is not used in Anglican currency and therefore have not included it elsewhere in the text, while yet acknowledging it on ecumenical and biblical grounds in the title.[8]

---

[1] It is difficult to see why this passage should be thought to be particularly appropriate.

[2] Ps. 119.33-38.

[3] Ps. 145.1-7, 21.

[4] Ps. 119.165-174.

[5] However much we may insist on the concept of corporate personality or of the collective ego, the Psalm at the ordination of a bishop sounds altogether too much like the candidate's protestation of his worthiness for the office.

[6] But Synod itself then took a grammatical point and amended it again to '. . . Priests (also called Presbyters).'

[7] *op. cit.* p.9.

[8] GS 327Y, §12.

In effect, then, the theological *status quo* is maintained and Küng appears as a left wing radical even by Anglican standards. But it has to be admitted that Küng would not appeal to most Anglo-Catholics and the revisers have to contend with pressure from them as well as from more protestant groups.

It may be thought that the provision for vesting is significant of a move towards a more sacerdotalist view of the ministry. It is difficult, however to make the charge stick. In the first place it is a question of making liturgical provision for what is a widespread practice anyway, namely the vesting of the deacon or priest with the stole. In the second place, it is not a compulsory provision, being mentioned only in a permissive note at the beginning of the service. Thirdly, the note suggests that vesting take after the Declaration, not after the imposition of hands, so that it is clear that it is not to be regarded as an essential part of ordination. Indeed, it reforms the existing practice.

Furthermore, the phrasing of the Note 'Where it is agreed . . .' was designed specifically by the revision committee

'in order to cover both the authority of the bishop to order the service and the scruples of the candidates in matters not universally accepted.'[1]

It is to be hoped that account will be taken of such scruples, although it should at the same time be recalled that the revised Canons of 1969 repudiate any theological significance attached to particular items of vesture.[2] As it is no very edifying spectacle to have some candidates vested and others not, nor a thing to be admired that one party should impose its will on others, we can perhaps hope that sensitive bishops will be met by sensitive candidates and that vesting with the stole in the appropriate manner may be recognized as a way of signifying the whole office to which the candidate is to be ordained and not simply as a symbol of a eucharistic role or, worse, of an assertion of the priority of the sacraments over against the priority of the word.

Similarly, by a narrow majority, the revision committee decided to make the *porrectio instrumentorum,* or tradition of chalice and paten to priests, and pastoral staff to bishops, a matter for agreement. Synod itself added '(the chalice and paten)' and '(pastoral staff)' to the revision committee's opening Note.

In the long run, however, the most significant section of the services for the assessment of doctrine must be the Declaration. Concerning the ministry of deacons, Series 3 adds to their responsibilities as described in 1662 inasmuch as he is to 'search out the careless and indifferent'. We may discern here a greater stress on the evangelistic task of the ministry which also finds expression at other points.[3]

[1] *Ibid.* §19.
[2] Canon B.8.
[3] As, e.g., the final question put to candidates and the prayer following the imposition of hands. (cf. *The Documents of Vatican II,* p.47, 'Among the principal duties of bishops, the preaching of the gospel occupies an eminent place').

There is no doubt that the Roman Catholic understanding of the episcopate, as expressed in Vatican II, is that it is 'the apex of the sacred ministry'[1] with the priesthood acting in an assistant capacity. Series 3 does not use the sacerdotal language of Vatican II but it does describe the bishop as 'chief pastor' and the priest as called to work 'with the bishop and with his fellow priests.'[2]

Concerning the order of priest, the Declaration contains the bulk of the material of which the 1662 homily consisted, albeit in a more concise form and without 1662's stress on the dire consequences of negligence. It is prefaced by a brief description of the role of the priest to parallel that of the deacon. The revision committee rejected a proposal to revise the first paragraph 'so that the function of a priest might be seen to be presiding at the celebration of the Holy Communion' preferring instead the original logical sequence of proclamation, repentance, absolution, baptism, confirmation, Holy Communion.'[3] Above all the priest is to set before himself the Good Shepherd 'as the pattern of his calling, caring for the people committed to his charge, and joining with them in a common witness to the world.'

A bishop, as chief pastor, is called to lead in serving and caring for the people of God, co-operating with them in oversight, with a special responsibility for promoting the unity and mission of the Church.[4] In one respect it may be thought that the bishop's role has been weakened. While Series 3 is in accord with 1662 in insisting that his administration of discipline must be characterized by both firmness and mercy, there is no great emphasis, as in 1662, on his task of banishing all erroneous and strange doctrine. But it must be added that the bishop is seen in a positive rather than a negative light: his task is to uphold the truth of the gospel against error rather than simply to banish error. We might say that he is to be an apostle of the truth rather than a heresy hunter.[5]

The question of the doctrinal stance of the Church of England *vis à vis* Scripture, the creeds and the 39 Articles has to be seen in the context not only of this declaration but also of the Declaration of Assent which both deacons and priests have to make (but which only bishops make during the service). There will undoubtedly be some critics who will feel that there has been a grave weakening of the position of the Church of England in dispensing with the very direct 1662 form 'Do you unfeignedly believe all

[1] *Ibid.* p.41.
[2] Series 3 contains no suggestion of the doctrine of Vatican II that the episcopate is to be regarded as 'the fulness of the sacrament of Order.' Significantly a proposal to introduce a similar concept, with the consequent problems of assessing its meaning, was rejected by the revision committee. (GS 327Y, p.48).
[3] It would have been out of harmony with the theology of the Roman Catholic rite and Vatican II, which regard the episcopate, for example, as a pastoral charge. So J. D. Crichton: 'The liturgy . . . is the pastoral service of God's people.' *(Christian Celebration: The Sacraments* (Geoffrey Chapman, London, 1973), p.144).
[4] cf. the ARCIC statement *Authority in the Church.*
[5] Perhaps to make the point clearer, the revision committee added 'to uphold the truth against error' to the declaration and 'from error and false doctrine' to the litany.

the canonical Scriptures of the Old and New Testament?' but equally little doubt that to the vast majority the two questions which replace it will seem adequately rigorous and in practice more susceptible of interpretation and application. The second question, concerning the doctrine of the Church of England is to be viewed strictly in the light of Canon A.5 and the Declaration of Assent. If this is done, it should not be as vague as at first sight may appear.

At one point only in the service is there a sacerdotal note, but even that has been set squarely within the context of the priesthood of the whole Church. In the prayer continuing from the laying of hands on priests, the bishop says, 'Set *them* among your people to offer with them spiritual sacrifices acceptable in your sight and to minister the sacraments of the New Covenant.'[1]

[1] See the commentary p.21 below, for a further discussion.

3. COMMENTARY

(1) The Notes

Notes 1-3 place the Church of England firmly within the ancient traditions of the western Church. Ordination takes place with prayer and the imposition of hands and, in accordance with the *Apostolic Tradition* of Hippolytus, hands are laid on the deacon by the bishop alone, on the priest by bishop and presbytery, and on a bishop by those bishops who are present[1] (a minimum of three including the archbishop of the province being required). It is the kind of detail that may well escape the layman's attention altogether; its significance is almost certain to. Any change, however, would need adequate justification and so it is probably best left as it has been.

According to *Apostolic Tradition,* hands are laid on the deacon by the bishop alone because he is not being ordained to the priesthood but 'to the service of the bishop.' It is to differentiate him from the presbyterate since 'he does not share the counsel of the presbyters but administers and informs the bishop of what is fitting.'[2] Clearly the logic of *Apostolic Tradition* is no longer relevant, since a deacon is no longer regarded as an assistant to the bishop, although some symbolic differentiation may be of value. It might even be argued by analogy with the practice for the ordination of a priest that hands should be laid on candidates for the diaconate by other deacons, for *Apostolic Tradition* argues that hands are laid by the presbyters not in order to ordain the candidates for the presbyterate, but to put their seal on the ordination, by way of confirmation or ratification. In this way they signify their approval, and welcome a brother to the presbyterate.[3] On the other hand, Hippolytus could be quite wrong in his assertion that priests do not ordain.[4]

Note 4 leaves open the question of the form and conduct of the service as a matter to be determined by the bishop. It was suggested to the revision committee that rubrical directions concerning the positioning of candidates and their participation in the communion should be added. In placing the responsibility on the bishop, 'having regard to tradition and local custom' the committee expressed the desire that 'Bishops should give sympathetic consideration to requests from candidates as to the form of service to be used (e.g. whether 1662 or the modern form).'[5]

The ancient tradition that ordination should take place within a eucharistic setting is maintained by Series 3, note 5 making clear that any authorized form of service of Holy Communion may be used. It should perhaps be added that it would seem preferable that Series 3 should be used to avoid a sudden change in language and atmosphere.

1 *Ap. Trad.,* 2, 7, 8.
2 *Ibid.,* 8 ('[he receives] that which is entrusted [to him] under the power of the bishop.' H. B. Porter, *The Ordination Prayers of the Ancient Western Churches* (Alcuin/ S.P.C.K., 1967), p.11).
3 cf. ARCIC *Ministry and Ordination,* para. 16.
4 He may be rationalizing a practice that antedates the emergence of episcopal precedence. It is interesting to note that hardly a single writer in the Elizabethan period explicitly denied priests the right to ordain. (Bradshaw, *op. cit.* p.43). In the CSI rite presbyters join in laying hands on candidates for the episcopate. But again see Bradshaw in *Essays on Hippolytus.*
5 GS 327Y, §16.

With respect to notes 7 and 8, attention has already been drawn to the significance of the phrase 'where it is (so) agreed' and to the position of the vesting in the service.[1]

(2) The Ordination of Deacons

Series 3 follows the unanimous practice of the Church of South India, the Anglican-Methodist Ordinal and the Roman Catholic order (hereafter called the Pontifical) in abandoning the confusing Prayer Book practice of referring to the making or ordering of deacons,[2] the ordering of priests, and the ordaining or consecrating of bishops. Instead it speaks of ordination in each case, adding 'or consecration' in the case of a bishop.[3]

The earliest pattern of ordination would appear to have placed bishops first followed by priests, and then deacons followed by minor orders. The reasons for the reversal of orders are obscure and need not concern us greatly, but may be connected with (a) the gradual movement towards a view of the diaconate as a stepping stone to the presbyterate[4] and (b) a similar movement towards a view of the deacon's liturgical role as that of reading the Gospel rather than that of 'offering the gifts'.

It is to be noted that a service has been provided for the ordination of deacons and priests together, a useful addition which should save both confusion and page-turning.

(3) The Collect[5]

The same collect, redrafted by the revision committee is used in each service and expresses more clearly than the original the context of the ordained ministry within the ministry of the whole people of God. It contains petition both on behalf of the Church at large and for those about to be ordained in a way that does not confuse the two.

(4) The Ministry of the Word

The Series 3 Holy Communion convention of three lections, Old Testament, Epistle and Gospel, is observed, with the provision of psalmody, but attention should be drawn to Note 6 giving the presiding bishop discretion to choose alternatives to the Old Testament and Epistle lections. Comment has already been made on the readings set, but we should note that both the Epistle and Gospel at the ordination of deacons have been taken over from

[1] See p.13 above.

[2] The opening rubric of the 1662 service speak of deacons 'to be ordained', in addition to 'making' in the title and 'ordering' in the page headings. The Sahidic version of *Ap. Trad.* uses *kathistanai*, meaning 'appoint' in the case of a deacon, which could conceivably amount to evidence *against* the use of 'ordain'. But the same word is used to mean 'ordain' in *Ap. Trad.*, 8, while the Latin text uses *ordinare* throughout.

[3] 'Consecrate' is also used in the text of the service for a bishop.

[4] Only the Ethiopic text of *Ap. Trad.* contains this idea, in a prayer that the deacon 'may attain the rank of a higher order.' The Latin Roman liturgy as found, for example, in the Leonine or Gelasian sacramentaries contains a similar petition (*The Ordination Prayers of the Ancient Western Churches*, p.35).

[5] Note that from this point on the order of sub-headings represents the order of the material within the respective rites. The only variation from this is that, when deacons and priests are ordained together, the deacons are presented, then the first part of the Declaration from the deacons' rite is read (i.e. the 'job description' of the deacon), then the priests are presented and the full Declaration from the priests' rite is read (with the deacons joining the priests in responding to the examination); later, after the Prayers, first the Deacons are ordained and receive their New Testaments, then the priests are ordained and receive their Bibles.

the Anglican-Methodist Ordinal, the Gospel at the ordination of priests is a section of the same passage in the Anglican-Methodist Ordinal, while the Gospel at the ordination of a bishop is the same as that both of 1662 and the Anglican-Methodist Ordinal.

(5) The Presentation

The form of the Presentation strives to be faithful to the actual processes of the Church of England in selecting ordinands and also to involve the congregation without asking the people to make judgments based at best on second-hand evidence.[1] The ancient response *'dignus est'* may be appropriate where the ordinand is well known to the congregation but scarcely appropriate to the 20th century Anglican situation, where the candidate may come from another diocese altogether. Moreover that response is apt to place more stress on the worthiness of the candidate than on the calling of God. The CSI rite contains the question 'Do you trust that these persons are, by God's grace, worthy to be ordained?' with the response 'We are, to God be the glory.' The same form is used in the Anglican-Methodist Ordinal, while the Pontifical has the formula 'We rely on the help of our Lord God and Saviour Jesus Christ and we choose our brother here present for the office of deacon' with the response 'Thanks be to God'. It can be seen, then, that while the Series 3 formula owes its concept to these predecessors and to the ancient practice of the Church, in form it owes nothing. Moreover, the people are asked not only for their approval, but also if they will uphold the candidates in their ministry.

No opportunity is offered for impediment to be alleged since, in the first place, it is covered in a more positive manner by the questions put to the congregation and, in the second place, the revision committee itself commented 'With the extensive vetting of candidates we see no need of an opportunity to show impediment.'[2]

One further welcome addition should be noted, namely the inclusion of the name of each candidate and of the place where he is to serve. In this way each individual is given an identity, a particularly valuable feature where the number of candidates is large.

(6) The Declaration

As already observed the Declaration now has a standard form, opening with a 'job description' which owes much to 1662 but relocated so that the questions follow naturally from it.[3] As this section has already been discussed at some length with respect to its doctrinal significance, I shall at this point draw attention only to some features of the Declaration in relation to other rites.

Concerning the first question, the revision committee turned down a proposal to redraft so as to enquire about the motives of the candidate in seeking ordination along the lines of the CSI rite on the ground that 'ordination is a response to a call to enter the Ministry'[4] but did include a phrase drawn from that same rite 'so far as you know your own heart'.

[1] The departure from the form used for deacons and priests in the service for a bishop is necessary to reflect the present practice concerning the election of a bishop.
[2] GS 327Y, §36.
[3] It is interesting to note that the homily in the Pontifical is not to be regarded as a fixed text. (J. D. Crichton, *op. cit.*, pp.140, 151, 159).
[4] GS 327Y, §40(b).

The second question is identical to that of the Anglican-Methodist Ordinal (which itself took its form from the CSI rite) but replaces the final phrase 'and as the supreme and decisive standard of faith' by 'through faith in Jesus Christ.'.

The third question is largely dependent on the Anglican-Methodist Ordinal. 'Doctrines', plural in the original report, becomes singular in the revised form, in order to bring it into line with Canon A.5 and the Worship and Doctrine Measure.

The fourth question contains, as might be expected, a variation appropriate to the ordination of a bishop. It is, nonetheless, noteworthy that, following the Anglican-Methodist Ordinal, the bishop himself is asked if he will 'accept the discipline of this Church', which may be taken, perhaps, as indicative of a desire to express the servant character of the ministry.

The fifth question is drawn from 1662, as reflected in the CSI and Anglican-Methodist rites, except that at the revision stage the phrase 'and fit you for your work' was altered to read 'and fit you to uphold the truth of the Gospel against error.'

The sixth question, absent altogether in the Anglican-Methodist Ordinal, owes little in form to any of its predecessors. The original ending '. . . to be an example to the people of God' was amended to the present 'according to the way of Christ.' Christian behaviour is, after all, not primarily a matter of 'being a good example', but of discipleship of Christ.

Question seven has no parallel in the 1662 deacons' rite, but is drawn essentially from the priests' and bishops' rites, with the added emphasis on unity of the CSI bishops' rite. This emphasis on unity had a particular importance for the Church of South India with its diverse roots in the various traditions, but equally it is relevant to the Church of England in its wide-ranging diversity and more particularly in its present ecumenical relationships.

Question eight in the deacons' and priests' rites is drawn from the Anglican-Methodist Ordinal, which itself leans heavily on the CSI rites. The question put to the bishop is the only one that is totally different from those put to deacons and priests, reflecting appropriately the bishop's responsibility as chief pastor, while at the same time not separating him from those among whom he lives. Indeed, there is here an impressive emphasis on his responsibility for leadership in evangelism and we may perhaps suppose that the tasks referred to in the 1662 rite ('will you be faithful in ordaining, sending or laying hands upon others?') are to be seen as subsumed under this more general heading as a part, but only a part, of the larger responsibility.[1]

A form of prayer standard to all the services concludes the Declaration, drawn, with minor changes, from the Anglican-Methodist Ordinal, itself a shortened version of the collect at the end of the 1662 priests' and bishops' examinations. It has always been odd that no concluding prayer is offered for the deacon in 1662; the insertion therefore is a welcome innovation.

---

[1] The possible reasons for the insertion of the question into 1662 are discussed by Bradshaw, *op. cit.,* p.92.

Two points remain to be made about the Declaration. First we must note again that in contrast to 1662, the questions for deacons and priests are identical, and differ only slightly for bishops. They are to be seen, therefore, largely as questions concerning the foundations of the Christian ministry, not as concerning the particular duties of the individual offices. Secondly, the section is entitled 'The Declaration': the 'examination' within it is formally necessary, but is not of course the basis for selection for ordination, and the title indicates the chief thrust of the section.

(7) The Prayers

The lengthy form of the litany in the 1662 services has led to its omission or abbreviation, a practice readily understood, even if it is to be regretted. The shorter form in Series 3 should, therefore, be widely acceptable. It is now, moreover, an integral part of the prayer of the people, contained in a single section. The confusing practice of a double 'prayer of the people' is avoided and the service given a clear and logical sequence.[1] The concluding prayer was amended by the revision committee to meet a criticism that it was inadequate as a penitential prayer in a service which otherwise contains no penitential section.[2]

(8) The Ordination

Strictly speaking, we should regard this part as one prayer in three sections, the middle section accompanying the laying on of hands.[3] The whole prayer is too lengthy to be recited over each candidate, while the alternative, the imposition of hands in silence, has been rejected. Those therefore who wish to see in it a 'moment of consecration' will do so, but the general atmosphere of the services militates against the concept, inasmuch as it expresses the conviction that ordination is the work of God

The first section, identical for priests and bishops, retains the reference to Eph. 4.11f contained in 1662, but otherwise prefers the imagery of the CSI and Anglican-Methodist Ordinals (the latter being the model at this point), echoing in turn 1 Pet. 2.9; Heb. 3.1; 1 Pet. 2.25; Heb. 2.14. The parallel passage in the deacons' rite, an amended version of the passage in the CSI and Anglican-Methodist rites, echoes Phil. 2.5-11 and Mk. 10.43-45.[4] Curiously, Series 3 follows CSI in omitting references to the 'ransom for many' which is included by the Anglican-Methodist rite. The prayer, thus, in the deacons' rite reflects the Gospel reading's emphasis on service, while the prayer in the other two services focusses on the variety of ministries given by God to his Church.

In each case this section ends with the same thanksgiving formula, including the phrase 'whom we ordain in your name.' Originally included in the following section, this phrase was transferred on the ground that it 'made for an awkward reading', but it is to be welcomed inasmuch as it reflects a matter on which the preface to the CSI Ordinal is adamant, namely that, strictly speaking, it is God who ordains.[5] The transference of the phrase, now permits undivided attention on the prayer being offered.

[1] cf. Bradshaw, *op. cit.*, pp.190, 211.
[2] GS 327Y, §45.
[3] The text of these prayers is to be found in Appendix 1 (pp.26-27).
[4] The Gospel reading is Mk. 10.35-45.
[5] The point is repeated in the second sentence of the examination in the CSI service for presbyters and bishops. Compare the proper thanksgiving to Series 3 and *The Lambeth Conference 1958*, p.88.

In common with all the modern ordination rites Series 3 abandons the imperative form 'Receive the Holy Ghost . . .', using instead a single form for all three orders. It is most particularly to be welcomed that the same formula is used for deacons as for priests and bishops.

The continuation of the prayer, following the imposition of hands, is individually composed for each order, drawing again on the CSI and Anglican-Methodist rites. The section in the deacons' service is particularly rich in biblical allusion, containing echoes of, at least, Eph. 3.17; Rom. 15.13 and Heb. 10.22. The section in the priests' service contains a small but important amendment by the revision committee, consisting of the insertion of the phrase 'with them' before 'spiritual sacrifices'.[1] The omission of this phrase at the Report stage is particularly strange because both CSI and Anglican-Methodist rites contain the words 'with all thy people.' It has to be admitted, however, that the whole clause remains somewhat ambiguous. The prayer in the service for bishops is the longest of the three, perhaps rather heavily didactic in character. It contains a reference to 2 Cor. 13.10 drawn from the prayer prior to the imposition of hands in 1662.

The revision committee turned down a proposal that the Roman Catholic practice of anointing the palms of the newly ordained priests should be adopted at this point, on the ground that Synod had been asked for, but not yet given, its mind on the use of chrism in general.[2] But in any case such a practice at this juncture would seem inappropriate: quite apart from the obscurity of its meaning, it would suggest that anointing is itself an essential aspect of ordination. Vesting has been moved from this position, it would seem, to make precisely that point; to introduce unction would be to restore the confusion, unless it were accompanied by some carefully worded formula, similar perhaps to that of the Pontifical.[3]

(9) The Giving of the New Testament/Bible
It is presumably as a hangover from the giving of the Book of the Gospels, from which the deacon would read, exercising his diaconal responsibility, that the newly ordinaed deacon is given a New Testament. There seems to be no other reason, and even that, it must be said, is a poor one. It would seem a great pity that the Commission did not bring themselves to follow the CSI and Anglican-Methodist rites in offering a Bible.[4]

In each case, the exhortation accompanying the giving of the book is appropriate to the order, that for the bishop containing a direct quotation from 1 Pet. 5.4. The exhortations to deacons and priests are substantially those of the CSI rites, that to deacons being particularly notable in that it ignores the 1662 liturgical responsibility for reading the Gospel. The exhortation to the newly ordained bishop, however, differs considerably, in

[1] See p.15 above.
[2] GS 327Y, §52.
[3] cf. J. D. Crichton, *op. cit.* p.137.
[4] At the Petertide 1978 ordinations at Ely, a deaconess was admitted together with the deacons, every feature of the service relevant to her being identical to that for the deacons, except that a cross was hung around her neck and she was handed a full Bible!

that it is framed wholly in a positive form.[1] In the original Report the first two sentences were said at the giving of the Bible, the remainder at the giving of the pastoral staff. Since this latter is now optional the two passages have been conflated[2]; the staff would, if desired, be presented in silence at the end of the exhortation. However, the principal feature of all three exhortations is that they do not constitute a giving of an authority not previously received; rather they look back to the meaning of ordination.

(10) The Communion

In line with the existing Series 3 services propers have been provided. The proper thanksgiving, completely rewritten at revision, speaks directly of ordination as the work of God, a wholly appropriate reminder while yet couched in a concise form suited to the thanksgiving as a whole. A post-communion collect, translated from the Roman Missal and added by the revision committee, contains a further petition on behalf of the newly ordained, while the proper blessing concludes the service by again setting the ordained ministry within the context of the ministry of the whole Church as the gift of God.

[1] It is related to 1662, as are the CSI and Anglican-Methodist exhortations, but with very considerable differences.
[2] A similar change took place between the 1550 and 1552 Ordinals.

4. PRACTICAL CONSIDERATIONS

In recent years there has been a trend towards decentralization not only in respect of government but also in the matter of ordinations. Many ordinations, particularly where there are few candidates may take place in a parish church rather than in a cathedral. While this may mean a certain loss in the diocesan and wider dimensions of ordination it is a distinct gain for the parishes. The cathedral may be some considerable distance from the parish or inconveniently situated where communications are poor. These factors, combined with the small capacity of some cathedrals, mean that only relatively few members of the congregations among whom the newly ordained will serve may be present, whereas there is little reason for them not to be present if ordinations are small scale affairs taking place on a local basis. In addition, the occasion may gain in significance for the candidates.

It may be that there is a strong case for more decentralization of this sort to take place. Is there any reason in principle why a deacon should not normally be ordained in the parish church ,symbolizing both his ordination to the ministry of the whole Church, by the presence of the bishop, and to the ministry of this particular congregation ? Priests might, perhaps, continue to be ordained in the cathedral in order to enable the presbyterate to lay hands together on the candidates and thereby to reinforce the wider context of ordination. Alternatively the ordination of priests could take place on a deanery basis.

While such a system would inevitably increase the work load of bishops it would seem unlikely that the increase would be very great. Indeed, there is evidence that it is already a system in practice, albeit on a modest scale. The diocese of London usually holds one ordination in St. Paul's and one in a parish church each year, alternating between Petertide and Michaelmas, while an examination of the Petertide ordinations for 1978 reveals that in Salisbury diocese deacons were ordained in Salisbury Cathedral but priests in parish churches, with never more than two candidates on any occasion. A generous supply of suffragan and assistant bishops does, of course, make such a practice more feasible.

The problems presented to the observance of Ember seasons would not be great, as dioceses have already adapted themselves to the preferability of Petertide to Trinity. Similarly, the difficulties relating to ordination retreats should not be insuperable. While it has been customary for candidates to go direct from retreat house to cathedral, it is scarcely a matter on which it is necessary to establish an inflexible rule. Indeed, it may be questioned whether it is a helpful practice at all for married candidates. More than one wife has commented on the burden of being left alone in a strange parish, to cope single-handed until reunited with her newly ordained husband.[1] To separate husband and wife in this fashion may not only be insensitive to

[1] I am informed that in at least one diocese it is customary for the family of the candidate to share in the retreat. Unfortunately, many diocesan houses are adapted only to a monastic existence.

the needs of the wife (and family) but calls into question the attitude of the Church to the wife's participation in her husband's ministry. On the one hand, much is expected of a clergy wife, not necessarily in her direct contribution to the parish, but certainly in support of her husband and by her hospitality at home, but on the other hand there is little recognition of the importance of her contribution. It should not be impossible to find a way for wives to participate more fully. In the first place, husbands and wives could be reunited before the service; in the second, they could be incorporated into the service itself. At an important psychological and spiritual moment for the whole family, on whose willing sacrifices the whole enterprise may have in large part depended, it is important that, in principle, the wife, if not the whole family, should be involved as more than spectators from a distance. The sensation engendered by the ordination of the husband alone has been desribed as an 'unmarrying'. If the ordination of a deacon were to take place in the parish church there should be no difficulty in making suitable arrangements.

The trend towards ordination in parish churches occasioned proposals to the revision committee that rubrical directions should be supplied concerning the positioning of candidates and their participation in the communion, but the committee decided to leave such questions to those involved. There is, of course, no reason why there should not be thorough consultation with the parish priest to ensure that arrangements are satisfactory. Clearly, where a man is to be ordained in his own parish church, it is desirable that he should participate in some way. A deacon or priest may equally be involved by reading one of the lections and/or by assisting with the administration.[1]

Not only is there a trend towards the ordination of deacons and priests in parish churches, there is also a trend towards the ordination of bishops in their own cathedral. This feature has led to the suggestion that enthronement might suitably follow on ordination without unduly lengthening the service. Such a move is clearly desirable but a present impossible because a newly ordained bishop is required to do homage to the Queen before he can be enthroned.[2] There is much, too, to be said for dispensing with the term 'enthronement', redolent as it is of the prince-bishops of the past and suggestive of an improper triumphalism. The alternative ,'inthronization', is hardly an improvement and it may be that 'installation', which has been used, will become more popular.

If the Series 3 ordination services are used in conjunction with Series 3 Holy Communion, there should be no problems in the conduct of the service since they are designed to gear into one another. Similarly, no problem should be presented by the use of Series 1 and 2 Revised. If 1662 is used, it would make sense to take up the Communion service at the *Sursum Corda*. Except where there is a nave altar or similar arrangement, the whole of the

---

[1] There is, after all, no special significance in the administration of bread and wine. Both in the Anglican and Roman Catholic Churches lay assistants are becoming increasingly common.

[2] GS 327Y, §56.

service to this point can take place at the entrance to the chancel or at the front of the nave, the candidates occupying, as is customary, the front seats.[1]

If priests and deacons are to be ordained in the same service, there is no reason why candidates for both orders should not come forward at the same moment for presentation, remaining there for the declaration which they can make together. At the laying on of hands candidates may go to the bishop or the bishop to the candidates (both practices are current) and if the candidates' families are to be involved it could be in one of the following ways:

(a) The deacon's wife (and possibly children) kneel with him while hands are laid on him. For obvious reasons it would be more difficult in the case of a priest.
(b) The candidates' wives (and children) are gathered in a suitable place alongside the candidates.
(c) The wives (and children) receive communion together with their husbands.

Concerning the vesting and *porrectio instrumentorum* attention must be directed to the notes at the beginning of the services. Where vesting is to take place it is to be after the declaration and, with two or more to assist with the task and the candidates standing, could be done in a minimum of time and fuss. Where the candidates are to be handed a chalice and paten special care must be taken .If the candidate has been given (and not handed back) the Bible, he cannot also be expected to juggle with the chalice and paten. But if he has handed back the Bible, should he not also hand back the chalice and paten lest an unfortunate piece of symbolism be read into the action ? Much to be preferred, if there is to be any handling of vessels, is the practice of the Pontifical, where the *porrectio instrumentorum,* with what Crichton calls its heavy emphasis on the priesthood as a cult ministry, has been abandoned. Instead, the bishop presents to each priest the chalice and paten already prepared, as the gifts of the people to be offered to God (*pace* Buchanan, Grove Liturgical Study 14). They do not accept the chalice and paten as a token of a priestly office. Rather they receive the gifts of the people in order that they may fulfil a liturgical function to which they have been called by ordination.[2] More simply still, the newly ordained could be involved in the preparation of the vessels.

By extension the giving of the pastoral staff has the same sort of significance in that it looks back to the meaning of ordination: it is not an essential part of the ordination itself, nor is it in any sense a conferring of authority.

---

[1] At a recent ordination in Durham, the imposition of hands took place in the sanctuary, virtually out of sight of the congregation. This is a practice wholly to be deplored, not least because of the way in which the action is divorced from, and indeed alienates, the congregation.

[2] *op. cit.* p.151.

APPENDIX 1: THE ORDINATION PRAYERS

The following are the actual Ordination Prayers from the three rites:

(a) Deacons

The candidates kneel before the Bishop; he stretches out h.s hands towards them, and says:

We praise and glorify you, most merciful Father, because in your great love of mankind you sent your only Son Jesus Christ to take the form of a servant; he came to serve and not to be served; and taught us that he who would be great among us must be the servant of all; he humbled himself for our sake, and in obedience accepted death, even death on a cross; therefore you highly exalted him and gave him the name which is above every name.

And now we give you thanks that you have called *these* your *servants,* whom we ordain in your name, to share this ministry entrusted to your Church.

Here the Bishop lays his hands on the head of each candidate, and says:

Send down the Holy Spirit upon your servant *N* for the office and work of a deacon in your Church.

When the Bishop has laid hands on all of them, he continues:

Almighty Father, give *these* your *servants* grace and power to fulfil *their* ministry. Make *them* faithful to serve, ready to teach, constant in advancing your gospel; and grant that, always having full assurance of faith, abounding in hope, and being rooted and grounded in love, *they* may continue strong and steadfast in your Son Jesus Christ our Lord, to whom, with you and your Holy Spirit, belong glory and honour, worship and praise, now and for ever.

The people say: **Amen.**

(b) Priests

The Bishop stands with the priests who assist him; the candidates kneel before him; he stretches out his hands towards them, and says:

We praise and glorify you, almighty Father, because you have formed throughout the world a holy people for your own possession, a royal priesthood, a universal Church.

We praise and glorify you because you have given us your only Son Jesus Christ to be the Apostle and High Priest of our faith, and the Shepherd of our souls.

We praise and glorify you that by his death he has overcome death; and that, having ascended into heaven, he has given his gifts abundantly, making some, apostles; some, prophets; some, evangelists; some, pastors and teachers; to equip your people for the work of ministry and to build up his body.

And now we give you thanks that you have called *these* your *servants,* whom we ordain in your name, to share this ministry entrusted to your Church.

Here the Bishop and priests lay their hands on the head of each candidate, and the Bishop says:

Send down the Holy Spirit upon your servant *N* for the office and work of a priest in your Church.

When the Bishop has laid hands on all of them, he continues:

Almighty Father, give to *these* your *servants* grace and power to fulfil *their* ministry among those committed to *their* charge; to watch over them and care for them; to absolve and bless them in your name; and to proclaim the gospel of your salvation. Set *them* among your people to offer with them spiritual sacrifices acceptable in your sight and to minister the sacraments of the New Covenant. As you have called *them* to your service, make *them* worthy of *their* calling. Give *them* wisdom and discipline to work faithfully with all *their* fellow-servants in Christ, that the world may come to know your glory and your love.

Accept our prayers, most merciful Father, through your Son Jesus Christ our Lord, to whom, with you and your Holy Spirit, belong glory and honour, worship and praise, now and for ever.

The people say: **Amen.**

(c) Bishops

The Archbishop stands with the bishops who assist him; the Bishop-elect kneels before him; he stretches out his hands towards him, and says:

We praise and glorify you, almighty Father, because you have formed throughout the world a holy people for your own possession, a royal priesthood, a universal Church.

We praise and glorify you because you have given us your only Son Jesus Christ to be the Apostle and High Priest of our faith, and the Shepherd of our souls.

We praise and glorify you that by his death he has overcome death; and that, having ascended into heaven, he has given his gifts abundantly to your people, making some, apostles; some prophets; some, evangelists; some, pastors and teachers; to equip them for the work of ministry and to build up his body.

And now we give you thanks that you have called *this* your *servant,* whom we consecrate in your name, to share this ministry entrusted to your Church.

Here the Archbishop and other bishops lay their hands on the head of the Bishop-elect, and the Archbishop says:

Send down the Holy Spirit upon your servant *N* for the office and work of a bishop in your Church.

The Archbishop then continues:

Almighty Father, fill *this* your *servant* with the grace and power which you gave to your Apostles, that *he* may lead those committed to *his* charge in proclaiming the gospel of salvation. Through *him* increase your Church, renew its ministry ,and unite its members in a holy fellowship of truth and love. Enable *him* as a true shepherd to feed and govern your flock; make *him* wise as a teacher, and steadfast as a guardian of its faith and sacraments. Guide and direct *him* in presiding at the worship of your people. Give *him* humility, that *he* may use *his* authority to heal, not to hurt; to build up, not to destroy. Defend *him* from all evil, that as a *ruler* over your household and *an ambassador* for Christ *he* may stand before you blameless, and finally, with all your servants, enter your eternal joy.

Accept our prayers, most merciful Father, through your Son Jesus Christ our Lord, to whom, with you and your Holy Spirit, belong glory and honour, worship and praise, now and for ever.

The people say: **Amen.**

APPENDIX 2: THE COMMON ORDINAL

Reference is made in this booklet to the Ten Propositions on unity, to which in 1978 the various Churches in England have been responding. The text of Proposition 6 includes the words '. . . and we agree that all subsequent ordinations [i.e. subsequent to the inauguration of the covenant and the 'recognition' of existing ministries] shall be according to a Common Ordinal which will properly incorporate the episcopal, presbyteral and lay roles in ordination.' The use of such an Ordinal would be comparable to that intended for the 1968 Anglican-Methodist Ordinal: to ensure that a common understanding of ordination and a common recognition of those being ordained was entrenched in the covenanting Churches. It would, if adopted, necessarily entail the abolition of existing Ordinals in the covenanting Churches, as it would have to be used for *all* ordinations, and not just be left for bishops who happened to like it to use as an occasional variant on their denominational use.

During 1977 the Churches' Unity Commission responded to requests for clarification from the Churches, and issued (amongst other 'Explanatory Notes') a document on 'The Common Ordinal' (May 1977).[1] In part this is concerned with two different ways ('Method A' and 'Method B'[2]) by which bishops could be involved in the ordinations. There is then a lengthy Preface (not to be read at ordinations), and the basic elements of a service for the ordination of presbyters.[3] These are: Service of the Word, Presentation, Examination, and Ordination. The 'Ordination' section includes a hymn invoking the Holy Spirit, then the ordination prayer itself. This prayer follows both the structure of the Series 3 prayer (i.e. with the laying on of hands in a context of prayer, accompanied by prayer, coming halfway through the main prayer), and in many points the wording also. Finally there is the optional delivery of a Bible and the optional giving of 'the right hand of fellowship'. Apart from the omission of the litany, the difference from Series 3 is minimal.

The 'Explanatory Notes' are in no sense part of the Propositions to which the Churches have been responding, but an indication of the further work which the Commission is undertaking ready for a favourable response to the Propositions. At the time of writing the Roman Catholic and Baptist Churches and Congregational Federation have indicated they cannot proceed on the basis of the Propositions, whilst the Anglican, Methodist, Moravian and United Reformed Churches have indicated that they accept the Propositions as in some way a basis for further consultation towards the 'Covenant'.

[1] The text of 'The Common Ordinal' is to be found (with other relevant material) in J. Huxtable *A New Hope for Christian Unity* (Fount, Collins, 1977), or in GS Misc 77 (May, 1978), the document presented to the Church of England General Synod in July 1978 (obtainable from the Church House Bookshop, Great Smith Street, London S.W.1.).

[2] 'Method A' involves the non-episcopal Churches adopting the historic episcopate, and is the method accepted by the Church of England in responding favourably to the Ten Propositions. 'Method B' involves Anglican (or other) bishops taking part in the ordinations in non-episcopal Churches.

[3] There could not be a service for the ordination of bishops, because under 'Method B' no *common* ordination of bishops would occur. On the other hand, it is difficult to see what distinctive *episcopal* role there would be for the 'visiting' bishop in the ordination of a presbyter by this Ordinal under 'Method B'. The denominational 'President' would preside (and speak the prayer). The bishop would simply be one of several ministers who assisted in silence at the laying on of hands.